D0984902

INSIDE THE WORLD'S MOST FAMOUS INTELLIGENCE AGENCIES

Inside Russia's SVR:
The Foreign Intelligence Service

Stella Suib

The Rosen Publishing Group, Inc.
New York

Published in 2003 by The Rosen Publishing Group, Inc.
29 East 21st Street, New York, NY 10010

Library of Congress Cataloging-in-Publication Data

Suib, Stella.
Inside Russia's SVR: the Foreign Intelligence Service/by Stella Suib.—1st ed.
p. cm.—(Inside the world's most famous intelligence agencies)
Includes bibliographical references and index.
ISBN 0-8239-3816-6 (lib. bdg.)
1. Sluzhba vneshni razvedki Rossiiskoi Federatsü—Juvenile
literature. [1. Russia (Federation). External Intelligence Service. 2.
Intelligence service—Russia (Federation). 3. Espionage, Russian.]
I. Title. II. Series.
UB251.R8 S85 2003
327.1247—dc21

2002012247

Manufactured in the United States of America

Cover: The building in the background is the Lubyanka, former headquarters of the KGB. In front stands a graffiti-encrusted pedestal that once held a statue of Felix Dzerzhinsky, founder of the Cheka, the forerunner to the KGB. The statue was toppled in 1991 by demonstrators after a failed attempt to overthrow Mikhail Gorbachev. In 2002, the mayor of Moscow proposed restoring the statue to its place in the center of the city, over the protests of human-rights groups.

INSIDE THE WORLD'S MOST FAMOUS INTELLIGENCE AGENCIES

Contents

Introduction

Russia is a vast nation that spans two continents. It was ruled by czars of the Romanov dynasty from the seventeenth to the twentieth centuries. From the Russian Revolution in 1917 to the failed attempt to overthrow the government in December of 1991, Russia was the most powerful republic of the Soviet Union. The USSR (Union of Soviet Socialist Republics) was a communist country. Even after the dissolution of the USSR, Russia remains the largest country in the world, nearly twice the size of the United States. The country includes seven time zones. It takes seven days by train to travel from Moscow, Russia's capital city in the western region, to Vladivostok, on the eastern edge.

In addition to its vast size, Russia is populated by many groups of people with different ethnicities and religions. Russians also have a variety of opinions about how the government should work. All of these things have led Russian life, past and present, to be filled with intrigue, action, and turmoil.

At the center of Russian life in the twentieth century were the activities and actions of the secret police, most often called the KGB. This group has had several names over the years. It has been reorganized many times. Some Russian leaders depended on the secret police to keep their governments strong, while other Russian leaders have tried to lessen the power of the secret police by reorganizing it.

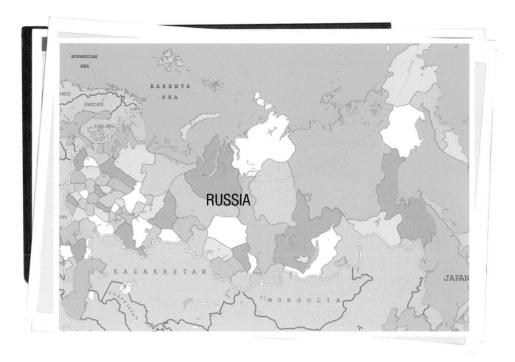

Russia is the largest country in the world. Russians comprised nearly half the population of the former Soviet Union. After the fall of the USSR in 1991, Russia formed the new eleven-member Commonwealth of Independent States, shown above.

Boris Yeltsin, president of Russia from 1991 to 1999, was a leader who wanted to reduce the strength of the secret police. When he came to power, he restructured the KGB, creating a new Ministry of Security composed of five new units.

The First Chief Directorate (the Russian acronym is PGU) was the KGB's department for collecting and processing foreign intelligence. Considered the best in the world by Russians, the image of the PGU as an intelligence superpower was enhanced by the media in the United States where it is often portrayed in books, movies, and TV as a cloak-and-dagger operation with invincible, patriotic agents.

Russia's foreign minister, Boris Pankin, has reportedly said that at one time nearly 50 percent of the Soviet people

Boris Yeltsin, president of the Russian Federation, gives the victory sign in Moscow on August 20, 1991, after helping to defeat an attempt by members of the Soviet government to overthrow leader Mikhail Gorbachev.

employed in the United States were working for the PGU, according to Gordon Bennett from the Royal Military Academy in Sandhurst, England. The FBI estimated the number to about 25 percent.

Lieutenant-General Leonid Shebarshin was the head of the PGU when the Soviet Union fell apart in the summer of 1991. Dismantling the KGB to protect himself, newly elected Russian president Boris Yeltsin set about to restructure Russia's police and intelligence operations. By December 1991, the PGU was reborn as the SVR (Sluzhby Vneshnei Razvedki), Russia's Foreign Intelligence Service. It was the first agency created by Yeltsin after the demise of the KGB. Shebarshin, formerly head of the KGB's PGU, become its director, but he soon resigned.

After an extensive search, Yeltsin named Yevgeniy Primakov to be the director of the SVR. Primakov answered directly to Yeltsin, the first time an intelligence agency would furnish daily information to the Russian chief. The KGB had kept most of its information to itself.

Chapter One

Intelligence at Work

In the United States, the responsibilities for gathering secret information at home and abroad are divided between two agencies—the Federal Bureau of Investigation (FBI), and the Central Intelligence Agency (CIA). For a long time in Russia, all spying activities were combined under one organization. Leaders of the Soviet Union believed that threats from citizens at home were as dangerous to Russia as threats from other countries. They also believed that the same methods should be used to investigate both domestic and foreign threats. As a result, Russia used the same organization and the same bugging techniques to gather information from foreign countries as it did to gather information about its own citizens in their homes or offices.

The KGB

The KGB, the Soviet Union's secret police, was like a state within a state. It had a rigid structure of leaders and agents who were very powerful. They often acted independent of the government. They made their own rules and were very secretive about them. The KGB was organized in departments known as directorates. Each directorate had its own

The exterior of the Lubyanka, which had been the headquarters of the KGB in downtown Moscow. This building currently houses the Lubyanka prison, the headquarters of the Border Troops, and the Federal Security Service (FSB) Directorate.

responsibilities. For example, Directorate "T" was responsible for fighting terrorism. The First Chief Directorate (PGU) was responsible for overseeing Soviet spies who collected intelligence, or information, from foreign countries like the United States and England.

Other KGB directorates were responsible for deep-cover spies, collection of scientific and technological intelligence, and monitoring Soviet citizens living in other countries to be sure they did not operate against their own government. The KGB Security Troops provided the KGB with the power to carry out its duties. These forces could protect the top leaders in the Kremlin, the seat of government in Moscow, and other key government buildings and people, or they could overthrow them.

Foreign Intelligence

As the foreign intelligence arm of the KGB, the PGU was considered elite even within the KGB. The PGU staff was composed of the best students from the most prestigious universities in the USSR. PGU agents were given their own housing, services, and facilities. Compared to most Soviets, they lived very well. It was this talented group that gave the KGB its reputation as an intelligence superpower.

PGU agents traveled to every country that was considered important by the leaders of the Soviet Union. They gathered information that might have political, economic, or technical value to the USSR.

The SVR is Born

When the Soviet Union collapsed in 1991, Russian president Boris Yeltsin dismantled the KGB to make sure the Soviet police would never again have absolute power. He was protecting his own position as well as the Russian people. To do the intelligence work of the PGU, he created the SVR, which reported directly to him. The SVR was not planned to function like the foreign ministry, which is part of the government, although SVR agents would be able to use the foreign ministry as cover for their work abroad.

Many of the newly hired SVR staff members had also worked for the KGB. And to date, all SVR directors have worked in the KGB. When Lieutenant-General Leonid Shebarshin resigned after a brief tenure, Yevgeniy Primakov became the next SVR director. Primakov had worked for the KGB as a journalist since 1957. His code name had been "Maxim." Writing for *Pravda*, the official Soviet daily newspaper, Primakov was an ardent supporter of Palestinian terrorists. Under Primakov, the SVR began to concentrate on issues that were more in line with the twenty-first century: the spread of weapons of mass destruction, international organized crime, industrial espionage, money laundering, and terrorism. Primakov has also been given credit for damage control in 1994 when American Aldrich Ames was exposed as a Russian double agent, much to the embarrassment of the SVR.

In 1996, Primakov was appointed Russia's minister of foreign affairs, replacing Andrei Kozyrev, who displeased the government because he admired Western democracies. Colonel-General Vyacheslav Trubnilov became the new director of the SVR. Having worked for the KGB for fifteen years in South Asia, in 1992 Trubnilov had become the SVR's deputy director. During his brief period of service, Trubnilov had to deal with several instances of SVR agents being exposed in Poland, Great Britain, Canada, and the United States.

President Boris Yeltsin resigned in January 2000, and Vladimir Putin was elected president of Russia in March. Putin had served as head of Russia's Federal Security Service (FSB, or Federal'naya Sluzhba Bezopasnosti). Just as the SVR is Russia's equivalent to America's CIA, the FSB is Russia's version of the FBI. By June 2000, Russian president Putin named Sergei Lebedev chief of the SVR. Lebedev had been a close associate to outgoing director Trubnilov.

Despite the aim of communism to provide for all its citizens, by 1990 many Russians became impoverished and homeless. Some, like this man, lived in makeshift shelters behind the Kremlin in Moscow.

Rising through the ranks of the KGB, Lebedev had become chief of an SVR Directorate. In 1998 he was shipped off to the United States as the official SVR representative to the U.S. intelligence community. In Russia this was considered an "honorable exile." According to Victor Yassmann, author of *The Future of Foreign Intelligence Under Putin*, the media has suggested that it is Lebedev's Western experience that appealed to Putin, who appears more interested in gathering Western intelligence than his predecessors, who were more focused on Asia.

Structural Secrets Revealed

Despite alleged Russian secrecy, information about the structure of the SVR is described on the Internet in the

On May 20, 2000, Sergei Lebedev was appointed director of the Foreign Intelligence Service (SVR) by order of president Vladimir Putin.

Intelligence Source Book. This organization reports that the SVR has headquarters in Moscow, as well as offices in Russian consulates, embassies, and places of business around the world. They report that the SVR is organized in a style similar to the KGB's First Chief Directorate, from which it is descended.

Within the SVR, there are three Directorates and three Services:

- Directorate "S" is responsible for top-secret agents around the world.
- Directorate "T" gathers intelligence about science and technology.
- Directorate "K" infiltrates other national intelligence and security services. It also monitors Russian citizens in other countries.
- Service "I" analyzes and distributes the information collected by SVR officers and agents. It publishes daily summaries for the Politiburo, the government body in Russia that sets policy. It also provides forecasts for the government about world developments.
- Service "A" plans and runs SVR activity.
- Service "R" evaluates the performance of the SVR abroad.

Spying Continues in Russia

When the Soviet Union dissolved in 1991 and the Cold War ended, it seemed that spying between Russia and the United States would lessen. Instead, it appears to be on the rise. Between 1991 and 1993, as reported by Congressional Research Service (CRS), there was "a 12 percent increase in intelligence collection efforts" by the SVR and the Russian military organization (GRU), who were afraid the United States would try to destabilize Russia's economy, which would have been a huge setback for the newest government.

Lebedev Speaks

The current leader of the SVR is Sergei Lebedev. CNN.com reported that in his first interview after being appointed in May 2000, Lebedev said, "Russia and the West faced the paradox of working with and against each other." He recognized that Russia and Western countries share the need to fight terrorism, drug smuggling, and the spread of nuclear weapons. He also claimed that the Russian people had no more to fear from the secret police, even though President Vladimir Putin and many of his staff are former employees of the KGB.

Those Who Tell State Secrets

Since its origins, the KGB was known for its brutal punishment of people it considered a threat to the state,

Investigative journalist Grigory Pasko *(right)* was arrested in 1997 by the FSB and accused of committing treason while working with Japanese journalists. He was sentenced in 2001 to four years of forced labor. Many believe that Pasko is being persecuted for exposing Russia's practice of dumping nuclear waste in the Sea of Japan.

both internationally and domestically. Its treatment, however, differed according to whom the people were and what type of secrets they were revealing. In 1991, *Moscow News* published an interview with General Oleg Kalugin, whose statements were seen as an embarrassment to the KGB. Officially, the KGB charged him with revealing state secrets. The authorities took away his general's stripes and his pension, but he did not go to prison. Despite the reforms in Russia, has much changed?

In fall 1992, the same newspaper published a story about a chemist who said Russia was producing chemical weapons. He was arrested for revealing a state secret and held in jail for ten days before he was allowed to see a lawyer.

Many members of the press continue to find themselves jailed for their investigative reporting and for the information they reveal. Russian reporter Grigory Pasko, a former Russian navy captain and reporter for the Russian navy's newspaper, was jailed for four years after being accused of spying for Japan. While reporting a story on a navy ship with the permission of the ship's captain, he filmed the crew emptying barrels of radioactive waste into the Sea of Japan. Russia was furious because it wanted to establish a good reputation with other nations in terms of environmental and nuclear issues.

In July 1999, a court found Pasko guilty only of abuse of office and granted him amnesty, or a pardon. On February 7, 2000, Pasko won a libel suit against the head of the Federal Security Services Pacific Fleet directorate, Nikolai Sotskov, who accused him of being a spy. A court awarded Pasko 25,000 rubles (about $870).

In 2002, the Kremlin backed the corporate hostile takeover of the independent Moscow television station NTV by Gazprom, a largely government-owned oil company. This meant that the government would be better able to control the information and programming aired by the television station.

Newspapers and radio stations that are viewed by the government to be disloyal to Russia by airing programs or comments that criticize the government or show Russia in a bad light find themselves hounded by tax inspectors, refused permission to print their newspapers on the government-owned printing presses, and forced out of their offices. Journalists who are viewed as troublemakers are assaulted or arrested.

Chapter Two

The Secret Police Rise to Power

For centuries, the Russian people had been ruled by leaders called czars. The czars, who were very rich, exercised absolute power over the Russians. Many people led lives filled with fear and terror.

Early in the 1800s, more than half of the czar's subjects—the people he ruled over—were poor farmers who were forced to work the land much like the slaves were forced to do in the United States. These farmers, called serfs, were bound to the czar and subject to his rule. Serfdom was abolished in 1861; nonetheless, many Russians remained poor and unhappy. Nobles and their families lived in luxury while many people starved in Russia. The working class, known as the proletariat, was forced to labor long, hard hours for very little pay. The people did not see the czar's government trying to improve conditions and their anger grew.

In 1903, the first military counterintelligence organization was created in Russia by the government of the czar as a reaction to foreign spies. At the beginning of World War I, the government under Czar Nicholas II expanded Russia's intelligence operations.

A portrait of the Russian royal family, the Romanovs, in 1915. From left to right, they are Marie, Czarina Alexandria, Alexei, Olga, Tatiana, Czar Nicholas II, and Anastasia. In 1918, they were secretly murdered by Bolsheviks during the Russian Revolution.

The Bolsheviks Step In

In 1917, Czar Nicholas II was overthrown in a revolution by the Bolsheviks and their leader, Vladimir Ilyich Lenin. The Bolsheviks had gone to factories and fields to encourage peasant and working-class people to challenge the rule of the czar's regime. When the government discovered these plans, they began to arrest Bolshevik leaders. Lenin went into hiding.

A two-year civil war followed during which the Red Army of the Bolsheviks fought the White Army loyal to Russia's ruling family, the Romanovs. The Red Army eventually won.

Lenin became the head of the first government. In 1921, Lenin introduced the new social and economic policy. It

Vladimir Ilyich Lenin speaks to soldiers in Red Square, Moscow, in 1919. Lenin introduced his own brand of communism to Russia. Although his career was short (from 1917 to his death in 1924), he created a model of dictatorship for Stalin, Mao, and Pol Pot.

I Spy

What do spies look for and why? Spies try to gather information about military secrets, new technology, and threats to their country or leaders. This information is called intelligence. Spies want to protect their country and give it advantages over other countries.

was called communism. The idea behind communism is that all goods and property are owned in common and are available to all who need them.

Once the czar was gone, the people expected that the Communists would make their lives better. But living conditions did not improve much in Russia. The government still had supreme power over the people and no one was permitted to own land.

Just weeks after taking power, the Bolsheviks founded the first Soviet intelligence agency, the Cheka, also called the All-Russian Extraordinary Commission for Combating Counterrevolution and Sabotage. In 1922, the Communists established a union composed of Russia and its neighboring countries, such as Ukraine and Georgia, that they called the Union of Soviet Socialist Republics (USSR, or the Soviet Union). For many decades, the Russian people lived under strict Communist rule.

Soviet Intelligence Becomes Central

Felix Dzerzhinsky, notorious head of the Cheka, instigated the "Red Terror," a program of capturing, torturing, and killing anyone that the Soviet regime considered a threat.

From its beginnings, the Communist leaders of the Soviet state believed that they were engaged in a life-and-death battle with capitalism and the non-Communist world. Espionage became a critical tool in the struggle for survival.

Over the years, Russian espionage agencies have had many names, including Cheka, GPU, OGPU, and NKVD, until the KGB was established in 1954. Despite the changes of names and leaders, the main purpose and brutal methods of the espionage agencies changed little throughout Soviet history.

Soviet intelligence has always directed its efforts toward the dangers of capitalism and betrayal at home and in other countries. Capitalism, which emphasizes free trade and private ownership, is at odds with communism, which is based on collective ownership of property and governmental control. The two systems, which create vastly different ways of life, have always seemed to threaten each other, perhaps because each felt intimidated by the existence of the other. The Soviet agents spied on foreign powers with the same ferocity with which they spied on their own people.

The KGB was an integral institution of the Soviet state since it was established by Nikita S. Krushchev in 1954. It was created to replace the People's Commissariat for Internal Affairs (NKVD). Between 1954 and 1991, the KGB amassed the strength and resources that enabled the government to maintain tremendous power over Russia and its people.

The structure of Soviet Communism, aided by the Soviet secret police, created a very rigid life for the people in Russia, eliminating private business, market activity, and property rights for citizens. The government seized property, usually by using force. The Communist Party confiscated property and possessions in order to issue them for collective, or shared, use. Often, however, the seized property was only used by Soviet rulers. Sometimes the government sold the possessions of citizens for hard currency, or for money from countries outside of Russia. Tens of thousands of people were arrested and murdered.

Working closely with the Communist Party, the KGB was also able to amass its own tremendous wealth. Some people believe that the KGB made money by having ties to organized crime. At the height of its power, the KGB had more than 500,000 employees, or agents. When most Russian people were suffering from poverty and the devastating effects of war, the KGB was alive, well, and strong. This made the Russian people fearful. They resented the KGB and its power.

Brutality of the Secret Service

From its beginnings, the Soviet secret service was primarily focused on domestic issues of security. During the two-year

Joseph Stalin (1879–1953) was dictator of the USSR from 1929 until his death. Under his regime, Soviet Communism was transformed from its revolutionary roots, which were based on human equality, into an authoritarian system of government. After helping defeat Hitler in World War II, Stalin established communist regimes across Eastern Europe by using brutal oppression and terror.

civil war following the Bolshevik Revolution, the Cheka used brutal methods to "defend the people" from counter-revolutionaries. There were many reports of the use of horrible and painful tortures in these early years.

The Secret Police Help Those in Power

Lenin believed the Cheka was the most important institution of the government. The secret police could help protect the Bolshevik one-party state from any opponents that threatened the Communist system. Perhaps because they had been instrumental to the revolt that overthrew the czarist government, both Lenin, and Joseph Stalin after him, believed very strongly that Western governments and Russians loyal to the former czarist government were conspiring to topple the new Bolshevik regime. The Cheka under Lenin and the NKVD under Stalin defended the Bolsheviks against all potential enemies.

Stalin and the NKVD Spread Fear

Joseph Stalin was a tyrannical dictator in the Soviet Union. The Soviet people feared Stalin because he was heartless and vicious. In 1928, he launched a program that took farmland from many poor farmers and claimed it for the government. Farmers were no longer allowed to grow food for themselves or for their families. Instead, they were forced to farm for the "good of the country." The government set quotas for farmers that determined how much grain farmers had to grow for the government to avoid punishment. Any man, woman, or child caught taking even a handful of grain meant for the government could be killed. Adding to the misery of the new lifestyle, there was a famine in 1932. Many farmers became very impoverished. Without enough food to eat, millions of people, especially in the Ukraine, died.

Stalin was convinced that many Russian people were conspiring to remove him from power and overturn Communist rule. Between 1934 and 1938, Stalin set out to rid the country of those whom he suspected of being enemies of the people. The NKVD assisted Stalin by doing the dirty work that would reinforce his power.

Millions of Russians were put in jail or labor camps called *gulags*, exiled, or shot. Stalin deported many prisoners to labor camps in Siberia, an isolated and deadly cold area of northern

Leon Trotsky, although a friend of Lenin, predicted that the revolutionary leader's ideas would lead to a dictatorship. After being banished from Russia, Trotsky was killed by a Stalin follower in 1940.

Russia. Many people died in the camps from exhaustion and disease. Conditions were so terrible during this period that Stalin's rule has been called the Great Terror of the 1930s.

Stalin and Trotsky

Stalin, in particular, used the NKVD to solidify his position as ruler by wiping out anyone or any group that could pose a challenge to him. One example was Leon Trotsky, who was the Commissar for War under Lenin. After Lenin's death, Trotsky's role in the Soviet government began to decline. However, Stalin believed Trotsky and his followers posed a major threat to his power in the Soviet Union. Stalin exiled Trotsky in 1927. Even though Stalin had sent Trotsky away, Stalin remained convinced that Trotsky and his followers were plotting against him. Trotsky criticized Stalin and his associates loudly and often, but with little power. In 1937, Trotsky moved to Mexico to protect himself from Stalin's wrath and suspicions. In 1939, Stalin personally instructed the deputy of foreign intelligence to send a task force to Mexico to assassinate Leon Trotsky. Trotsky had become the number-one enemy of the state—ahead of even Adolf Hitler and the Nazis, who were in the process of overrunning Europe, murdering millions of Jews and other innocent groups of people. In 1940, a trusted member of Trotsky's entourage, who turned out to be a Russian secret agent, killed him with an ice pick.

Leaders who came after Stalin continued to persecute those they thought threatened the Soviet state, although they used less police terror. Instead, they sought to gain popular support by relaxing the tight controls of the past. However, the KGB remained a very powerful institution for decades. Because it threatened their power, many secret police leaders actively resisted the changes that were introduced in the following decades.

Chapter Three

Successes of Russian Intelligence

A great success for the secret police came in the 1940s when it was able to recruit what became known as the Magnificent Five. Five young British students studying at Cambridge University in England were very interested and supportive of communism. They did not view communism as an evil force, like many citizens in the West at that time. The men were Donald Maclean, Guy Burgess, Anthony Blunt, John Cairnneross, and Kim Philby. After graduation, all the men rose to high positions in the British intelligence service, called MI6. Kim Philby would become the most notorious member of the group.

Philby is considered to have been the most successful and damaging Soviet double agent of the Cold War period. After being recruited into British intelligence in 1940, he went on to become head of counterespionage operations for MI6. He devastated the Western espionage network when he provided the Soviet Union with information that led to the deaths of many Western agents. One of his greatest successes was thwarting a plan being hatched by Britain and the United States to send groups of anti-communists into Communist-ruled Albania in 1950. As a

The KGB was best known for the successes of its foreign agents. Pictured above are some of the most famous—Blunt, Burgess, Philby, and Maclean—who, along with John Cairnneross, the Soviets dubbed "the Magnificent Five." These British men worked for the KGB not because they had been bribed or blackmailed, but because they believed in communism.

result of this information, when the nationalists crossed into Albania, the KGB was waiting. The Western agents were all killed.

In 1949, Philby was sent to Washington, D.C., as the top officer between British and U.S. intelligence services. While there, he learned that British intelligence agents were becoming suspicious of his friends from college, Guy Burgess and Donald Maclean. He warned Burgess and Maclean and they fled to Moscow before being found out and punished by England. Philby was suspected of being the person who tipped them off, but because there was no hard evidence, he was just asked to resign. He fled to Russia in 1963.

George Blake— KGB Master Spy

Convicted Russian spy George Blake in 2001 after presenting a book of letters exchanged between himself and colleagues also imprisoned in Britain. The book was published with support from the Russian Foreign Intelligence Service (SVR).

George Blake became another double agent who was highly damaging to British intelligence operations. Born in Holland, as a young man he fought against the Nazis with the Dutch underground resistance. He was captured by the Gestapo, the Nazi secret police, and placed in an internment camp in 1940. He quickly escaped and returned to fighting in the resistance. Eventually, he joined his mother and sister in London, where they had fled to escape the Nazis.

Once in England, he signed on with the Royal Navy. Accepted by the Special Operations Executive, he was sent as an espionage agent to Nazi-occupied countries in Europe to work with underground fighters against the Germans. In 1944, his job was to translate and interpret secret German documents.

After the war, Blake attended Cambridge University and studied Russian. Because of his skills and his excellent war record, he became an official member of the British navy's Foreign Office and was sent to a post in South Korea. When

American soldiers load a howitzer during the Korean War. The war began in 1950, when the Communist North Korean army invaded South Korea. The United Nations sent in troops, mostly American, to help the army of South Korea defend itself. By 1953, with neither side close to victory, a truce was signed to end the conflict. The war added to the tensions between the U.S. and the USSR, which supported North Korea's Communist cause.

the Korean War broke out in 1950, Communist troops over-ran Seoul. Blake was taken prisoner. After being held for three years, he tried to escape. Blake was captured and put before a firing squad. He shouted in Russian that he was not a spy. The officer in charge of the firing squad, a Russian diplomat, spared him. The two spoke about Soviet Communist philosophy. This encounter had a big impact on Blake. He converted to Communism.

Upon his release, Blake requested that he be transferred to MI6, the British secret service, to become a secret agent. He was accepted. When posted to West Berlin in 1955, Blake's assignment was to infiltrate Soviet spy operations. He acted as a double agent, pretending to supply the Soviets with false Western secrets, while identifying the Soviet spies. He was, however, betraying Britain by revealing the identities of top Western agents in East Germany to the KGB. He was really a double agent for the Soviet Union.

Blake photographed secret documents in the Berlin offices of MI6 and turned the film over to his KGB contacts. His biggest accomplishment for the Soviets was to expose the existence of the Berlin Tunnel. The United States and Great Britain had dug a tunnel into East Berlin, allowing U.S. spies to tap Soviet communication lines buried there. When the KGB found out about it from Blake, they filled it in.

Blake later took a post in Lebanon, hoping to escape what he felt was rising British suspicion of him. When the MI6 realized that Blake was really a Soviet double agent, they didn't want him to escape punishment. They had a friend of Blake's convince him to take a high-paying job back in London. Blake went to what he thought was a routine interview, but instead he was taken into custody by the MI6. He admitted he had been a Soviet agent. He told authorities that he had embraced Communism in 1953 and had planned to spy for Russia at that time. "I justified it in my mind by believing that I was helping, in a small way, to build a new society . . . But I think it is never wrong to give your life to a noble ideal and to a noble experiment, even if it didn't succeed," Blake said in an interview.

He was sentenced to forty-two years in prison. However, he would not serve even six of those years. Blake was put in Wormwood Scrubs Prison, an old, run-down facility in London. He managed to kick out a poorly constructed window bar and escape. He hid for a few weeks in England until the KGB smuggled him to Moscow.

The Manhattan Project

Although the Soviet Union and the United States were allies during World War II, at the same time the Soviets engaged in active scientific and technical espionage in America. They wanted to

Klaus Fuchs, a German physicist, helped the U.S. develop the atomic bomb, but also supplied nuclear secrets to the Soviets.

learn the secrets of U.S. radio engineering and aviation.

The KGB's biggest accomplishment was to steal information from the Manhattan Project, America's secret program that developed the atomic bomb, named for its location at Columbia University in Manhattan. Most of the scientists who agreed to pass information to the Soviets did so out of ideological conviction, not for money. They agreed with the ideas and principles of communism. Klaus Fuchs, the key player in the spy ring, provided very valuable information to the Soviets in exchange for a few small gifts. Most of those who participated in this espionage action believed that it would foster world peace if the Soviet Union also had access to nuclear weapons.

In 1941, Soviet agents obtained a report describing early British plans to produce atomic bombs. By the end of

In 1953, Ethel and Julius Rosenberg were convicted by the U.S. of conducting espionage for the Soviets. Thousands of people believed the couple was innocent and demonstrated on two continents on their behalf. Nevertheless, on June 19, 1953, the Rosenbergs were executed in Sing Sing Prison.

1942, Stalin had decided that Russia must also have this weapon. Late in 1941, Fuchs, a gifted physicist, began to pass top-secret British atomic secrets to Russian agents. Fuchs continued to feed the Russians information even after he was selected to work on the Manhattan Project. Because of his influence, Russian intelligence was able to penetrate many areas of the Manhattan Project. They had agents reporting on uranium and plutonium research as well as agents who were involved in the construction of the plant and equipment being used on the Manhattan Project. Given the scope of the Nazi threat and the German alliance with the USSR, the U.S. and British governments were surprisingly unconcerned about hiring people who had communist backgrounds for highly-sensitive jobs.

Russia in Nuclear Trouble: Chernobyl

On April 26, 1986, in the Russian city of Chernobyl, a nuclear reactor exploded, releasing thirty to forty times the radioactivity of the atomic bombs dropped on Hiroshima and Nagasaki. Abnormal radiation levels were registered in Sweden (787 miles or 1,267 kilometers away) at one of its nuclear facilities.

The Chernobyl disaster and its impact on the course of Soviet events ranks as one of the greatest industrial accidents of all time. Thirty-one people died immediately. Hundreds of thousands of Ukrainians, Russians, and Belorussians were forced to abandon entire cities and settlements within the zone of the most extreme contamination. Estimates vary, but it is likely that three million people are still living in contaminated areas. Billions of rubles have been spent, and billions more will be needed, to relocate communities and decontaminate the rich farmland in the zone so food can once again be safely grown.

A May, 1986 view of the Chernobyl nuclear plant. One month earlier, it was the site of the world's worst nuclear disaster.

Chernobyl has become a symbol to many of the dangers of uncontrolled nuclear power. It also shows how the Soviet system is shrouded in secrecy and deception. Russia did not make the accident public—Sweden did. This shows a disregard for the safety and welfare of workers and their families living in the area

After the accident, many members of the Russian media found themselves hounded and threatened by the KGB for bringing more attention to environmental problems in Russia, especially those of a nuclear nature.

In exchange for immunity, David Greenglass testified in the 1950s espionage trial against his sister and brother-in-law, Ethel and Julius Rosenberg. Greenglass was sentenced to fifteen years for his part in passing information to the Soviets about the atomic bomb.

In addition to Fuchs, American communists were supplying NKVD agents with massive amounts of classified atomic secrets. The FBI believed that Julius and Ethel Rosenberg were running a spy ring for the Soviets in the United States. Ethel allegedly recruited an American communist named David Greenglass who was an electrical engineer and a believer in Stalin and the Soviet Union. In 1944, Theodore Alvin Hall joined the spy ring. Also a communist supporter, he, too, was convinced that an American nuclear monopoly would threaten world peace.

Nineteen-year-old Hall handed agent Lona Cohen the crucial secrets of America's atomic bomb, which she hid in a Kleenex box and carried across the country to Stalin's agents. Five months before the first test of the atomic bomb at Alamogordo, New Mexico, the Russians had put together information on all of the main elements of the bomb's construction. Most of this information came from Fuchs, Hall, and Greenglass. The first Soviet atomic bomb was detonated just over four years after the American test. It was an exact

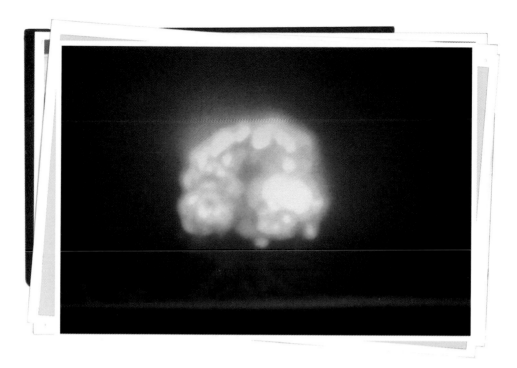

In 1939, Albert Einstein warned President Franklin Roosevelt that Nazi Germany was attempting to construct an atomic bomb that would be the most deadly weapon the world had ever seen. But it wasn't until the Japanese bombed Pearl Harbor in 1941 that the U.S. government established the Manhattan Project. This photo, from July 16, 1945, shows the first nuclear explosion, conducted by the U.S. in Almagordo, New Mexico. It cost the country $20 billion.

copy of the Alamogordo bomb. This established the Soviet Union as a nuclear power. From that moment on, the United States and the Soviet Union launched the Cold War, which would last from 1945 to 1991. Nuclear arms and the weapons race would continue to be a major issue facing the two countries into the twenty-first century.

Chapter Four

Attempts to Tear Down the KGB

Mikhail Gorbachev, who led the Soviet Union from 1985 to 1991, and his supporters, wanted to reform, or change, the government and lifestyle in Russia. The power of the KGB was threatened. If Gorbachev succeeded, the KGB would lose its power.

The reform efforts created confusing economic and political times. People in the Soviet Union had a variety of beliefs about how the government should behave. Some people badly wanted change; others wanted life to stay the same. Russia's manufacturing, farming, military, and central government, as well as its currency, the ruble, all suffered. Jobs were scarce. Fighting broke out between communities. Crimes big and small increased. People were frightened as the Soviet Union took steps toward a more democratic way of life.

The new Russian government that followed Gorbachev's, under the leadership of Boris Yeltsin, made several changes in the laws and organization of criminal justice after the dissolution of the Soviet Union in 1991. But the overall system of internal security has retained many of the characteristics of the original Soviet KGB.

On December 7, 1987, Soviet leader Mikhail Gorbachev met with American president Ronald Reagan in Washington, D.C., for a White House summit.

Gorbachev Introduces Glasnost

Gorbachev introduced *glasnost*, or political freedom, to a country that had a history of secrecy and few individual liberties. He also introduced *perestroika*, or economic restructuring, in an attempt to modernize the Communism that had dominated Russia.

Russia struggled in its efforts to build a democratic political system in which citizens could participate in the government. Gorbachev wanted a market economy to replace the strict social, political, and economic controls of the Communist period. He encouraged the Russian people to make money for themselves and their families—not just for the good of the government. He thought if the people had

In this photo from August 1991, a crowd in Moscow cheers for the Russian soldiers who backed Boris Yeltsin after Soviet hardliners failed to overthrow the government.

more money and were less afraid, all of Russia would improve. He could not have anticipated what these changes would mean to the life people had known for decades in the Soviet Union.

No Improvement in Russia

Reactions to Gorbachev's new policies were mixed. The changes he wanted rocked the foundation of long-standing, established pillars of the Communist Party as well as Russia's economy and society. While the changes did not replace the old ways entirely, newfound freedoms of assembly, speech, and religion, the right to strike, and multicandidate elections undermined the Soviet Union's authoritarian structures, as well as the familiar sense of order and predictability. Long-suppressed, bitter interethnic, economic, and social grievances led to clashes, strikes, and growing crime. With consumer goods as scarce as ever, civil unrest mounted and bloody crackdowns claimed lives. Instead of creating abundance for the people, food grew more scarce and food lines got longer. It was hard for Gorbachev to keep the peace in his country.

The KGB Tries to Take Over

On August 21, 1991, Vladimer Kyruchkov, head of the KGB, was arrested for trying to lead an overthrow of Gorbachev and his government. KGB staff began to destroy its own documents so they would not be made public by the government. The next day, Vadim Bakatin was appointed by Gorbachev to take over the KGB. Bakatin's first order was to stop KGB managers from

Vadim Bakatin at a Moscow press conference in August 1991. As the newly appointed head of the KGB, he was assigned by Gorbachev the task of dismantling the agency after the failed 1991 coup.

destroying any more important papers. Unhappy about the new leader, most KGB managers quit their jobs within two weeks.

On October 24, 1991, Gorbachev signed an order to abolish the KGB altogether. KGB responsibilities were assigned to other offices within the Russian government. Although many of these duties were given to new personnel, most of the people who were overseeing the new divisions had worked for the KGB. For instance, the new department, the SVR, which was established to monitor external intelligence, was placed under the direction of Evgeni Primakov. He had been a member of the KGB in the mid-1960s.

Spy Gadgets

Though the life of a spy may not be as glamorous as a James Bond movie, spies get to use some pretty neat gadgets.

- Satellites These powerful tools help spies see from a great distance and photograph the location of people, equipment, and buildings.

- Concealed Cameras When spies need to capture a photo without being noticed, these handy tools do the job. The Steineck ABC wristwatch, for example, was used during the Cold War. It could take pictures while an agent pretended to check the time.

These Russian spy gadgets include three miniature cameras, microfilm, and a cigarette pack that hides film.

- Dead Drop Spikes These spikes were stuck in the ground to hide information during a dead drop, in which a spy would go to a secret location and leave something for another spy. The spikes could hold money, small cameras, or film.

- Cypher Sheets Often messages were written in a secret code, or cypher, on these tiny pieces of paper so if they were found by the enemy, they could not be read. Some pages were small enough to fit inside a walnut shell.

- Pen Microphones Soviet spies used these devices to record conversations. It was easy to keep one in your suit pocket and talk into it without anyone noticing.

Boris Yeltsin and Russia in Trouble

On December 19, 1991, Gorbachev, in poor health, turned over power to Boris Yeltsin. Under Yeltsin's leadership, Russia embarked on even more far-reaching reforms, as the Soviet Union divided into fifteen republics to form the CIS, the Commonwealth of Independent States.

Economic and social conditions in Russia continued to decline. Its treasury could not afford to pay its debts to other countries. Russian government workers went without pay for months. The Russian people, once again, were unhappy with the conditions of their country.

It was a very uncertain time for Russia as some groups tried to take power away from Yeltsin. In addition to having serious economic problems, Russians from different ethnic groups were fighting against each other. The crime rate skyrocketed. Under these conditions, Yeltsin and his advisors had to rely on state security and internal police agencies to keep order.

Yeltsin wanted to create a new security structure that would be very different from the original Soviet KGB. He wanted to lessen its power and the grip it had on Russia and its government. But he still needed to be protected from political opponents. To improve life for the Russian people, he needed help to control the fighting, labor strikes, drug trafficking, and organized crime.

Yeltsin knew that he wanted a security service to continue to carry out counterintelligence against foreign spies who were working inside Russia. He also needed spies to tell him what was happening in other countries.

Many Russian people did not believe that the KGB was dead, especially when Yeltsin chose many former KGB officers as his top cabinet ministers. In addition, former KGB officers were chosen for important positions in his office, in state-run industries, and in the media. Many members of the Russian media, including newspaper, radio, and TV reporters, felt that Yeltsin was not committed to destroying the power of the KGB after all.

Chapter Five

Spies Still Going Strong

Aldrich Ames was an American who worked for the United States Central Intelligence Agency (CIA). His job was to uncover Russian spies. He became another of Russia's most successful double agents. Born in 1941 in Wisconsin, he started working for the CIA in 1969. Ames moved to Mexico City in 1981 and met his future wife, Rosario, a Colombian woman he later recruited for the CIA.

Ames began selling information to the KGB in 1985. By the time he was arrested in 1994, he had received more than $2.7 million from Russia in exchange for American intelligence information. Having identified American spies to Russia, he is blamed for the deaths of nine U.S. agents in Russia.

The arrest of Aldrich Ames was a major embarrassment for the SVR. It showed the world that they were spying on the United States at the same time they were negotiating peace. The United States was furious as well as indignant. Not only had Ames revealed many of America's technical secrets, most of the American agents who he had exposed in Russia had been shot.

To reaffirm the importance of the SVR, Boris Yeltsin visited the SVR headquarters in Yasenevo to speak with 800 staff members. According to Gordon Bennet, Yeltsin told SVR agents that while military budgets were being cut, intelligence information was more important than ever in protecting

CIA agent Aldrich Ames was arrested in 1994 by the FBI for having spied for the Russians since 1985. He pleaded guilty and received a life sentence.

Russia's security. Intelligence operations would increase. "Extensive use is made of the methods of secret diplomacy in the practice of international relations," he has reportedly said. "We should be able to look under the cover of these secrets so as not to be caught napping."

Primakov also authorized the first-ever report about Russian intelligence to be released. Called "New Challenge After the Cold War: Proliferation of Weapons of Mass Destruction," it urged the countries that owned nuclear weapons, including the United States, Britain, China, and France, to reduce their arsenals and better protect their dangerous material.

Primakov also backed the publication of a six-volume account of Russian civilian intelligence organizations. While his opponents say he revealed nothing new, he made a show of a new Russian openness. At the same time, he highlighted the importance of the SVR, and he may have attracted new, good-quality recruits. In the days of the KGB, agents lived lifestyles far above the average citizen. But the new SVR could offer its people none of those benefits. As a result, good recruits had been scarce.

Former Pennsylvania State University researcher Edmund Pope *(center)* was convicted in Russia of spying for the United States on December 6, 2001. Although Pope was sentenced to twenty years in jail, Russian president Vladimir Putin pardoned him.

When FBI veteran Richard Hanssen was arrested in the United States for selling secrets to the Russians, the story was covered extensively by the Moscow media as an example of the Russian-U.S. "intelligence war." According to Victor Yasmann, writing for the *Russian Reform Monitor*, many Russian newspapers told their readers that Hanssen had been revealed to the American government by a Russian diplomat, Sergei Tretyakov, who had recently defected to the United States. At the same time, Boris Labusov, spokesman for the SVR, told the Russian Information Agency-Novosti (RIA-Novosti) that the "tradition of his agency, as well as its counterparts in other countries" is not to comment on such news. Labusov is also reported to have said that "the SVR sees any intelligence activities as a form of protection of national interests."

Say "Cheese"!

The Soviets were very vigilant about keeping an eye on their own agents to be sure they were not tempted to become double agents.

One example is Oleg Penkovsky, an officer in the Soviet military's intelligence agency. He gave valuable information to the West during the Cuban Missile Crisis in 1962. Coming under suspicion for having an unauthorized meeting with a foreigner, Penkovsky was watched very closely by the KGB.

Oleg Penkovsky pleaded guilty in Moscow to charges that he passed Soviet secrets to a British and American espionage ring in 1961 and 1962.

The family that lived upstairs from his apartment was sent on vacation. The KGB drilled a hole in their floor so KGB agents could watch the comings and goings of Penkovsky through a pinhead camera. When the KGB had clear evidence of his spying, he was arrested, tortured, and shot.

At the end of the article, Yasmann noted that, "Remarkably, even before the Hanssen arrest, the weekly *Rossiya,* which is close to Evgenii Primakov's 'Motherland-All Russia' party, mentioned Putin's secret directive to intensify spy activity against the United States. This order apparently ordered Russian spy agencies to increase their political and military intelligence-gathering in the U.S.

In a farewell ceremony in December 1999 at the Kremlin in Moscow, acting Russian president Vladimir Putin *(left)* shakes hands with Russian president Boris Yeltsin, who had suddenly resigned. In March 2000, according to Russian law, an election was held in which Putin was elected president.

making Sergei Ivanov, the Secretary of the Russian Security Council, responsible for overseeing these efforts."

New Agents for the SVR

In 1992, Primakov visited the Moscow State Institute of International Studies. This school is considered to have Russia's largest group of students eligible for civilian intelligence work, according to Gordon Bennett in a report he wrote for Great Britain's ministry of defense in 2000. Soon after Primakov's visit, a Primakov spokesperson revealed that since the SVR did not have the same financial benefits or romantic identity that it had enjoyed when it was an intelligence service under the KGB, it had become difficult to attract high-quality recruits. To counteract these changes, he announced that the government would initiate a special course about the Russian Intelligence Service at the school. The goal was to attract twenty-five suitable graduates to the Foreign Intelligence Academy each year. Russian officers would give similar courses in other Moscow locations. Primakov is reported to have visited the Foreign Intelligence Academy several times over the next several years. In 1994, he sponsored educational reforms at the school.

Who is Admitted to the Foreign Intelligence Academy

Men between twenty-two and thirty-five years old, in good health, are eligible for the Foreign Intelligence Academy. They are expected to have completed their higher education, with excellent skills in languages and analysis. They must be well versed in political history, as well as have technical ability. Candidates, who must be Russian citizens, are asked to set their political beliefs aside when they enter the academy. The policy of the academy is that as long as a student does not try to promote his religion, it will respect a student's right to privacy. All students must take a lie detector test.

Course of Study

Students at the Foreign Intelligence Academy study intelligence operations, including methods of collecting information and technical analysis. They learn the basics of unarmed combat as well as how to drive a variety of vehicles. Students practice using guns and other basic firearms. They must take rigorous courses in the humanities, which include languages, philosophy, sociology, economics, and psychology. Foreign Intelligence Academy students study Russian and international art and literature, especially as it relates to their work in the field.

According to Gordon Bennett's report, Lieutenant-General Nikolay Petrovich Gribin, commandant of the academy, had expressed disappointment that new candidates arrive on campus lacking military service and adequate life experience. The teaching staff has been forced to find ways to help students fill these gaps.

The Benefits of Working for the SVR

While SVR agents earn much less than people working in Russia's private companies, the SVR can still offer them several incentives. In addition to receiving excellent educations, their jobs can be extremely stimulating, and their working conditions pleasant. They are paid on time, which apparently is an issue in Russia. SVR agents are often able to enter areas that are off-limits to even the wealthiest Russians. Work as an SVR agent often includes international travel.

The SVR vs. the CIA

The SVR of Russia and the CIA of the United States are most often at odds with each other, as one organization is discovered to be spying in the other. The CIA has continually spied in Russia, and five intelligence officers who were technology

In 1995, Russia sent its army to overpower rebels *(shown above)* in the republic of Chechnya. By 1996, 40,000 Russian troops had poured into the area and about 25,000 people were dead. In May of 2002, Russia set forth an amnesty agreement, though fighting continued.

specialists defected from Russia between 1991 and 1992. They revealed a great many Russian secrets, forcing the SVR to reorganize their methods of gathering scientific and technical intelligence. The 1994 case of American spy Aldrich Ames, in which he was revealed as a double agent for Russia, only made the situation worse.

But the Russians remain interested in fighting international terrorism and corruption, the drug trade, and the spread of weapons of mass destruction. A spokesman for then–first deputy director Trubnikov announced in 1997 that while cooperation between the SVR and the CIA was practically impossible, perhaps the FBI and the FSB (Russian's equivalent to the FBI) might work together if the presidents of each country could reach an agreement.

Inside Russia, the SVR and the FSB appear to be improving their interdepartmental communications by undertaking joint operations and analyzing problems that affect them both. But to deal effectively with international terrorism, corruption, and other serious world issues, as well as to improve its economy, Russia will have to cooperate with other countries. Russia has not been without its allies. India has proved to be a useful partner to the SVR because of its location close to China.

New Strengths for the SVR

Despite all of the changes in Russia and the SVR culture, the SVR remains one of the finest intelligence organizations in the world. As people who have grown wealthy through criminal organizations move to other countries, some are pursued by the SVR. Many of these Russians have moved to industrialized, democratic countries, obtaining permanent resident status or even new citizenship by making investments with stolen money or faking marriages. Knowing about their criminal backgrounds, the SVR can blackmail some of them into gathering secret information that is valuable to Russia.

Putin Urges the Secret Services to Roll with the Times

In a December 2001 speech, Russian President Putin urged the secret services to "apply their skills, honed in the repressive Soviet era, to defending democracy." Putin stressed that while the main purpose of the Soviet secret services had been to repress civil rights and freedoms, democratic reforms of the past decade demand that security agencies now work to defend democracy. FSB Chief Nikolai Patrushev said foreign intelligence agencies had expanded their positions in Russia, requiring more vigilance than ever.

Putin promised to help restore Russia's military, improve the economy, decrease poverty, and fight crime.

New Cooperation After September 11, 2001

On December 20, 2001, Sergei Lebedev, the head of Russia's SVR at this writing, gave a rare interview to the Russian newspaper *Trud*. Welcoming the new cooperation between Russia and the West, he doubted that it would last once the anti-terrorist campaign had ended. He acknowledged, however, that the events of September 11, 2001, created a real turning point for the world community. "Exchange of information between the countries of the world community now take place on a different, improved level," he said.

Lebedev received his intelligence training in the Ukraine, a former republic of the USSR. He worked in East and West Germany for twenty years, and was involved in its reunification. He has also worked in the United States. Russian president Putin appointed Lebedev to his current job in May 2000.

In his interview, Lebedev said that Russian young people were becoming more interested in working for intelligence services. "At the moment we are getting excellent guys," he reported.

In May 2002, U.S. president George W. Bush *(left)* visited Russian president Vladimir Putin in Russia for friendly meetings. In this photo, they have just arrived at Piskarevskoye Memorial Cemetery in Putin's hometown of St. Petersburg for a wreath-laying ceremony.

He also gave assurance that Russian intelligence agents had long since stopped using so-called exotic methods like "someone being run over by a car or pricked by an umbrella."

When asked about working with Russian president Putin, Lebedev said, "Naturally, the president's understanding of intelligence problems…makes it easy for me to talk to him. If I need to, I can speak to the president at any moment."

Help, Russian Style

The Russian government has long expressed concern about the spread of rebels and terrorism in Central Asia that they feel is supported by Osama bin Laden and the Al Qaeda terrorist network. They also believe that Afghan terrorists are financing their activities with money they earn through the narcotics trade. According to Stephen J. Blank at the Strategic Studies Institute, the "SVR and FSB have now revealed their past cooperation with Washington (in general terms) and appear ready to upgrade it."

They report that President Putin has already offered intelligence information to the United States from the SVR, and perhaps the FSB, to aid in the fight against terrorism and Osama bin Laden. Putin has reportedly opened Russian airspace to U.S. reconnaissance flights. He has also extended to the United States the secret use of former Soviet air bases in Central Asia for the staging of humanitarian flights.

However, he will not allow the United States to stage military missions from Russian military bases. At this writing, Putin is steering Russia clear of any military involvement with or support of the U.S. war on terrorism.

Glossary

Bolshevik A member of the extremist wing of the Russian Democratic Party that seized power in Russia as a result of the revolution in 1917; also known as Communist.

Cold War The ideological conflict between the United States and the Soviet Union between 1945 and 1991, carried on by methods short of war and without breaking off diplomatic relations.

communism A system of government that eliminates private property with the aim to create a stateless society for the good of all, governed by a single, authoritarian party.

counterintelligence Activities designed to block an enemy's sources of information or to deceive the enemy with misinformation.

coup The sudden overthrow of a government by a small group.

czar Emperor; one having great power and authority. The ruler of Russia until the 1917 revolution.

democratic Favoring social equality; a government in which people have an equal voice.

dictator A ruler who exercises total power that is harsh or cruel.

directorates The departments that comprised the original form of the KGB, or secret police.

espionage The practice of spying to obtain information about the plans and activities of an enemy, competitor, or foreign government.

exile   Forced removal from one's country or home.

famine   An extreme scarcity of food.

gulag   Labor camps in the USSR, widely used by ruler Joseph Stalin during the 1930s.

glasnost   A Soviet cultural and social policy promoted by Mikhail Gorbachev in the 1980s. A policy of openness in public discussions about current and historical problems.

intelligence   Information secretly gathered by spies about an enemy or possible enemy.

Kremlin   The stronghold of Moscow, Russia's capital, and the governing center of the USSR.

market economy   An economic system in which resources and production are privately owned, and prices, production, and the distribution of goods are determined mainly by competition in a free market.

perestroika   An economic and social policy introduced by Mikhail Gorbachev in the 1980s to transform the Soviet economy into one that is more open and market-oriented.

revolution   The overthrow of one government or ruler for another.

serf   A person forced to work the land and subject to the rule of a lord.

For More Information

Organizations

Embassy of the Russian Federation
21650 Wisconsin Avenue NW
Washington, DC 20007
(202) 298-5700

Russian Cultural Centre
1825 Phelps Place NW
Washington, DC 20008
(202) 265-3840

American Association for the Advancement of Slavic Studies
8 Story Street
Cambridge, MA 02138
(617) 495-0677
http://www.fas.harvard.edu/~aaass

Videos

Russian People—Revolution and Evolution. Directed by Ed Dubrowsky.
Video Knowledge Learning Library.

Web Sites

Due to the changing nature of Internet links, the Rosen Publishing
Group, Inc., has developed an online list of Web sites related to the
subject of this book. This site is updated regularly. Please use this
link to access the list:

http://www.rosenlinks.com/iwmfia/svr

For Further Reading

Brown-Fader, Kim. *Russia* (Modern Nations of the World). San Diego, CA: Lucent Books, 1998.

Corona, Laurel. *Life in Moscow*. San Diego, CA: Lucent Books, 2000.

Corona, Laurel. *The Russian Federation*. San Diego, CA: Lucent Books, 2001.

Fleming, Fergus. *Tales of Real Spies*. Newton, MA: EDC Publications, 1998.

Lamphere, Robert, and Tom Schachtman. *The FBI-KGB War: A Special Agent's Story*. Macon, GA: Mercer University Press, 1995.

Lerner Geography Department, ed. *Russia, Then and Now*. Minneapolis, MN: Lerner Publications Company, 1992.

Stickler, Jim. *Russia of the Tsars*. San Diego, CA: Lucent Books, 1998.

Bibliography

ABCNews.com. "The Threatened Bear." Retrieved February 20, 2002 (http://my.abcnews.go.com/PRINTERFRIENDLY?PAGE=http://abc-source.starwave.com/).

Al'bats, Evgenia. *The State Within a State: The KGB and Its Hold on Russia—Past, Present, and Future.* New York: Farrar, Straus and Giroux, 1995.

Badkhen, Anna. "Putin Announces Cabinet Shake-Up." *Boston Globe.* March 29, 2001.

BBC News. "Russians arrest CIA hacker." June 26, 2000. Retrieved February 2, 2002 (http://news.bbc.co.uk/hi/english/world/europe/newsid_806000/806984.stml).

Bennett, Gordon. "The SVR: Russia's Intelligence Service." March 2000. Retrieved August 20, 2002 (http://www.fas.org/irp/world/russia/svr/c103-gb.htm).

Chalmers, Rachel. "Cyberterrorism? Experts Question Russian Data Raid." October 8, 1999. Retrieved February 7, 2002 (http://www.findarticles.com/cf_0/m0CGN/3764/56194719/print.jhtml).

Cook, Chris. *The Facts on File World Political Almanac from 1945 to the Present.* Fourth edition. New York: Checkmark Books, 2001.

Corson, William R. *The New KGB, Engine of Soviet Power.* New York: Morrow, 1985.

Ebon, Martin. *KGB: Death and Rebirth.* Westport, CT: Praeger, 1994.

Fish, M. Steven. *Democracy from Scratch: Opposition and Regime in the New Russian Revolution.* Princeton, NJ: Princeton University Press, 1995.

Gannon, James. *Stealing Secrets, Telling Lies: How Spies and Codebreakers Helped Shape the Twentieth Century.* Dulles, VA: Brassery's, 2001.

Gevorkian, Natalia. "The KGB: 'They Still Need Us.'" *The Bulletin of Atomic Scientists.* Retrieved February 11, 2002 (http://www.bul-latomsci.org/issues/1993/jf93/jf93Gevorkian.html).

Jack, Andrew. "Shake Up Could Revive KGB." *Financial Times.* January 8, 2001. Retrieved February 21, 2002 (http://www.financialtimes/printthis.clickability.com/pt/printThis?clickMap=printThis&fb=Y).

Kim, Mi Won. "A Vote of Confidence: Russians Elect Vladimir Putin as Their Next President." *Time for Kids.* March 28, 2000. Retrieved September 13, 2002 (http://www.timeforkids.com/TFK/news/story/6260,49741,00.html).

Kozakavich, Michael. "Russia's SVR: The Leaner, if Not Meaner, Successor to the KGB's First Directorate." May 30, 1997. Retrieved August 15, 2002 (http://russia.jamestown.org/pubs/view/pri_003_008_003.htm).

Lowry, Betty. "Washington, DC: On the Trail of Notorious Spies." *Boston Globe.* June 3, 2001.

Maasarani, Dina. "A Spy in the FBI?" *Time for Kids.* February 21, 2001. Retrieved March 3, 2002 (http://www.timeforkids.com/TFK/news/printout/0,9187,100150,00.html).

Medetsky, Anatoly. "Russian Scientist Charges." *Washington Post.* October 6, 2000.

Tyler, Patrick E. "Russian Tycoon's Bombshell: Can It Be?" *New York Times.* February 8, 2002.

Waller, J. Michael. "Russian Spies Are Alive and Well." *Insight on the News.* March 8, 1999. Retrieved February 7, 2002 (http://www.findarticles.com/cf_0/m1571/9_15/54032769/print.jhtml).

The Washington Post Company. "Mr. Putin's Latest 'Spy'" *Washington Post.* December 27, 2001. Retrieved January 12, 2002 (http://washingtonpost.com/ac2/wp-dyn/A28482-2001Dec26?language=printer).

World News Network. "Putin Urges Russian Security Shift." January 18, 2002. Retrieved February 21, 2002 (http://www.worldnews.com/?t=print1.txt&action=display&article=11474553).

World News Network. "Russia Reports Spying by U.S. Foes." 2001. Retrieved January 16, 2002 (http://www.worldnews.com/?t=print1.txt&action=display&article=10971246).

Yasmann, Victor. "The Future of Russian Foreign Intelligence Under Putin." February 6, 2000. Retrieved August 13, 2002 (http://www.hri.org/news/balkans/rfer1/2000/00-06-02.rfer1.html#27).

Yasmann, Victor. "Whither Russian Foreign Intelligence?" *Asia Times Online.* June 6, 2000. Retrieved August 22, 2002 (http://www.atimes.com/c-asia/BF06Ag02.html).

Index

Credits

About the Author

Stella Suib is a writer living in Albany, New York.

Photo Credits

Cover © Peter Turnley/Corbis; p. 5 © 2002 Geoatlas; p. 6 © Reuters NewMedia, Inc./Corbis; p. 8 © Gary Trotter/Eye Ubiquitous/Corbis; pp. 11, 37, 38, 39, 50 © Peter Turnley/Corbis; p. 12 © Sergei Velichkin/Itar-Tass/Arcon TML; p. 14 © Vladimir Sayapin/Itar-Tass/Arcon TML; pp. 17, 22, 24, 27, 29, 31, 32 © Hulton/Archive/Getty Images, Inc.; p. 18 © Novosti/Corbis; pp. 20, 34, 40, 46 © Bettmann/Corbis; pp. 28, 47, 53 © AFP/Corbis; p. 33 © TimePix; p. 35 © Corbis; pp. 44, 45 © AP/Wide World Photo.

Layout and Design

Thomas Forget

Editor

Jill Jarnow